we are all strangers
to someone.
we are all stargazers
to something.
we are all looking
for both in our
humanness.

-z.k.d

STRANGERS
&
STARGAZERS

Poetry and Prose

By: Zachry K. Douglas

get in your car. roll the windows down.
turn up the radio. scream every word.
therapy is different for everyone.
it comes to us when we let go of what
we had been squeezing the life out of.
what we had been keeping inside,
hoping we could hide it long enough
before it consumed everything we had
become trying to fight it.

i still believe love makes us better
humans even if things do not go
as planned. it is at the center of
all things living and dead. it is at
the center of my longing, my curse,
my fucking ache. it is challenging
to imagine a point in my life where
it isn't who i am. even though i
have none to speak of at this time,
it is somewhere floating around
the cosmos, waiting and defying
all the odds to make its way to
me once again.

i've always been that kid in the driveway, waving goodbye to everyone he loves. i remain emotional over the sentiment that sometimes you never get to hear hello again from the person you care most about. everybody i meet impacts my life, regardless of their tenure during the duration of the visit. everyone is somebody to me, and that's why i respect my feelings. they hold me accountable when i feel incapable of doing what others fear will demote their pride.

you cannot continue taking on the emotional
burden of your loved ones or the relationship
you are in. if you decide to move on, it is their
responsibility. it's always been theirs, but maybe
you were only that to them, and once they
groomed you and made you who they needed,
it was normal for you; taking on baggage.
taking on feelings you never expressed.
holding in resentment. playing along just
to keep the air clear. that is not living. that is
not love. you can help them when they need
it, but you cannot take it all on. especially
when it upsets them that you're helping as
much as you should. once you leave, fucking
leave. do not come back when they are down
and out, begging for something else. you gave
them your best effort. you are not their doctor,
mother, father, caretaker. do not feed in and
give into their ability to control you. do not
give them another chance. that is what we call
narcissism. you are worth more than being
played for an enabler, for a nurse to a mindset
and rage not meant for anyone to receive.
we as humans have a difficult time deciphering
what is good and what is only good for a short
amount of time. i know you will do your best.
i know you will reach out to family or friends
if it should ever manifest into something more
than you have the strength for. we only get this
life once. spend your time with those who value
who you are and only take advantage of a moment
to kiss you more and often, with a love so fucking
precious, you are a true hero in their story.

i've never been good at staying for long periods of time. i've come to know that humans make the biggest of messes with your heart if you give them more than they deserve. it is something i am still learning and i am surprised i still have as much of my heart left as i do. it has been through war dealing with these lovers, but i will become something better because of it. you will not get the last laugh. only death can laugh at its own jokes and go on living in the midst of survival.

i take my breaths and bruises to the water, to the mountains, to the city where they are needed. i am less of a boy these days, though i still find retreat in sounds of conflict and confrontation. they have never been a strong suit of mine. i am at times too gentle to be a human. i am too small to be a man. i learn from others around me and dodge what i can on purpose just to get out of any situation that makes me cringe or adds anxiety to a life already ridden with enough of its weight to crush a galaxy and devour a black hole. i am too full of hope for someone who knows death this well. i am too stubborn to listen to anyone who thinks they know what is best for me. my ears have formed into walls and nothing gets through them that doesn't know how to love me. what i seek died years ago. maybe before religion tried to save me. definitely before my bones grew its thick skin, which is soft for anyone who has been killed before they knew how to love themselves. my abilities are useless if i am not giving. if i am not leaving pieces of me behind. if i am not present in every god forsaken moment without any type of love to hold me together. but still, i live. i am a life still deciding which season keeps me alive more than the other.

-freedom from my mind-

i have been beaten by your words. strangled by your haunting curse. spat on by your impassionate views. mishandled and misused for the last time by you. amassing a lifetime of abuse, i shall kick in the door to an island universe. i will swim with the angels and submerse my soul; rising from the waters, revived and whole.

-i was once a murderer to my own
life. but now, i am the gardener
with dirt on his hands instead
of the blood-

to those who feel too much:

the only thing that remains,

are the dreams we are brave

enough to chase down.

for if we should ever fall,

may they continue to

chase what we leave behind.

i'll always choose writing about love over anything else.
i could write you the saddest words and still make you
believe love can exist between the living and dying.
between death and rebirth. between the opening and
closing of hearts. it is all relevant and all connected.
i am not here by accident or just coincidence, and
neither are you. we are flowers planted and replanted.
we are puddles turned into oceans. we are the desert
during the driest of seasons, yet we still give life a
name. we still give life a chance at survival because
that's what we are here for; a fucking chance at
something real and unknown to make it our own.
it isn't complicated. it isn't astrophysics. it isn't a
quantum realm theory or dissecting a star and
making matter, matter more or less than just being
here. i know i won't live here in St.George for much
longer than my lease is keeping me here, because i am
a child of travel. i am too spontaneous. i am too
wandering. i am not all here when it comes to being
here. my life was made to outrun any thought of having
a family or being tied to one specific origin of living or
breathing. my body has been spread out over thirty-three
years and if i can have another thirty-three to keep
stretching out until i am flat across the universe, then i
will have made it. i will have made my time worthy of
being called a life. my bones were not made to grow
upward. i am a part of the tree of life, and it grows with
harmony and change. it takes me being this way to ever
be truly happy. it takes crossing off places before this
place crosses my name off of life's list to be fulfilled.
my date of birth was not my beginning. it was the ending
of who i was before i had this body. now it needs to be
released into whatever journey awaits me. now my ending
has reason. now my ending has new life. now it has a new
set of numbers for others so they know my unfiltered age.

when you look back on your life, i hope you keep walking forward and never regret why you are now living and breathing as yourself. i know you have had days where pain overtakes any happiness you own. i know love sleeps like a wild wave that has yet to dream. i know you're hurting. so many of us hurt and know nothing else. but you are someone else. something far greater than what it says about you in the middle of the night when you are trying to remember what it feels like to be one with the stars. you are mighty and seeking. you are not the grave you once dug. you are not the scars you made on your skin to see if you could feel more alive.
you are approaching the beginning. the first of a million beautiful breaths that will build you into a goddamn hurricane; a subtle force for whenever you feel low again. do not become your ache. become more and more love. become your own reason to showcase an unbreakable heart to the masses who want nothing more than to see your fault lines and watch them run.

everything comes and goes in life. waves and people have a lot in common. the further they go out, the chances of them returning transformed and willing to stay longer grows exponentially. they will greet you with the biggest of hugs until you are completely drowning in them. i guess we all have our own singular wave we are looking for; hoping to drown in it until it, too, has to go back out for changes to come. we never know how long we will have them, but once you do, stay with them a while and ask how they have been. humans do not ask other living things enough questions these days. everyone thinks death comes to us either way. but if you looked at the flower long enough and studied why it moves the way it does, you would see it just added another year to your life for being kind.

love is still something i believe in. no matter how many times it leaves, i am still hoping it stays. i am not asking for forever. maybe a few minutes of your time to talk about what we want from this experience. living with an open wound never does anyone any favors. it just makes us more of animal that's afraid of dying. it makes us more ruthless to anyone trying to help heal what has the potential to turn into a scar for another day. one more day of understanding. one more day of holding the fight back. one more day of resting your feelings and allowing yourself a chance at forgiveness to those who only want what is best for you. it is okay to hurt. i've been howling for the last ten years. i am still in recovery. the last woman, my ex-fiance, had to endure a lot of misery and unwarranted anger from me. along with several other accidents that she had nothing to do with. but i have grown since then. at least i think i have. in October of this year, i will have been sober for five years. clean and free from the drink. it already has been ten years since i got out of the Marines. my life has changed dramatically and drastically for the better. now it is time to move on again.
a warrior's mindset never ends. regardless of how many battles you lose or win. each has a lesson for you to carry with you for the rest of your life.

    adapt. overcome. conquer your fears.

one day i will trust myself around
love again, just as i am trusting
myself around humans today.
i know there is something out
there i am not yet prepared for,
but may my heart never carry
doubt or guilt about my abilities
and actions needed to survive.

in my healing, i've learned how to forgive those who have turned me into someone i am not. i am the responsibility to my thoughts and feelings. i fail often with it, but i am giving all i can to make sure i do not become them when they are not mine to have or believe in to be true. i am a mind still being developed by sweet sounds of war and nature. one must maintain balance if he or she should ever want more than constant battles being waged by a mind versus a heart.

love looks a lot like the sunset
tonight. more purples and blues
than ever before. it seems as
though the sky can be bruised,
too. there is endearing peace in
this feeling we share. i'll see you
tomorrow and talk about it
over a brand new day.

i am learning each day my capacity of love and pain. some days, i cannot help but to feel every fucking thing around me.

more times than not, it is on those days i learn how to forgive myself for things that didn't go the way i wanted them to.

beauty holds a country for all those seeking its truth. we are space holders. we are energy magnets. we are the living and dead to all who wish to know us, and our crazy bones.

i can still feel the day i was born.
it speaks of my mother softly and
with immense praise. i know life
wasn't always the easiest or best
of times with her, but she did
love me before anyone else ever
could. she found a way to love
someone she knew nothing
about unlike many who have
crossed paths with me. she kept
me alive, and i hope through
these words, i can keep her and
the love i have for her alive.

i still get nervous around people who have yet to experience life. they talk without ache in their voice. they speak behind words they don't believe in. they only step outside when it suits them. they have never leapt out into an unknown feeling. they simply discard anything that isn't to their liking. they just sit there with doors closed when a beautiful moon is on display for them to love. maybe they love differently. maybe they are just not for change. they watch the same flowers die each day, but make sure they drink first when thirst overtakes their bodies. love is a deathly game for fools and those who believe they are more important than what keeps our hearts alive.

no one will ever be able to give you what you
give to others. the faster you realize this part
of life, the easier it all will ultimately be for
you with your love moving forward.
patience may not love you back, but it
will be there for you when you need a
break from love and its chaos.

humans just want to belong to something.
sometimes it is love. sometimes it is pain.
sometimes it is nothing more than just a
feeling we get from someone who knows
nothing about us, but gives us a sensation
in the bottom of our stomachs that makes
our lives better because we knew the same
thing, but never spoke out loud about it.
they showed us that judgment is only
given to those who reach out and slap
it out of someone. all we want is nothing,
but everything when we have enough time
to consider how many years we have left
to make our own choices before all of it
is out of our hands.

i let the hurt in and welcome it. i am still listening and learning from my emotional injuries i have sustained over the course of my life. i am still comprehending how much human it takes to feel these emotions. i want to be this so i can help others when and if they need it for them to know they will never have to be alone for a single fucking second. there is not enough help going around these days. it takes a tragedy just for someone to open up about what hurts them what scares them, what they are without when empty is all they have had to know.

i need to remind myself how much we take for granted while death picks no bones with anyone. it still ends up being the finality and having the final say in this lifetime. i need to stop worrying about what i can't control. i need to focus and reign in what i can to better prepare myself for the adventures still out there waiting for me to hear my name.

all the devils know me. i once thought hell was my home, but it was merely me passing through another stage of my life. not every fire is for you. not every touch is meant to last. goodbyes and hellos are all the same when you do not know the sound of your own voice.

most days i forget what i
even look like. some days
i am reminded by the
emotions in me.

other days i am reminded
by the emotions in others.

as the birds find their way, i too, shall find mine. with wings made from broken suns and crumbling moons, i'll gather up all of my strength and take to the sky to fly beside a love that will never leave me behind. beside a love that will rise with me and take on the wild.

i was born a wanderer, and i will find myself where others never care to go. that will be a resting place for me, but never home. my soul deserves to travel the lands and take in the beauty constructed by those who felt the same urge to leave where they knew they would easily be forgotten and never known.

it's been a while since
i have felt this way.

this feeling of belonging
to something. this feeling
of belonging to myself.

this feeling of belonging
in my own company.

this feeling of not wanting
another war inside of me
to begin.

by the time my life ends, i hope to have loved, understood, and took as many chances as i could. i hope to have never caused as much pain as was given to me. i hope so much these days.

i hope.

love taught me how to be more of myself and not what others expected me to be or give. it still teaches me that in your absence. it will be my greatest teacher even when the lesson leaves me and goes away for good. i'll still listen and pay attention to the heart and soul rather than what it looks and feels like to others.

what love doesn't teach you, it reveals to you later in life when you are willing to accept not everything you do because of it will matter when it is over. we carry more than just each other's bones these days. we carry one another regardless of how it ends or begins. we each carry a moment, dying to be born again somewhere it truly and rightfully belongs. until a single breath becomes a hurricane, i am a calmness without force.

may we always believe in healing
ourselves before attempting a
rescue mission for someone else.
may we always hold onto our wings
before giving them shelter to someone
else who knows nothing about sacrifice,
but takes everything when they leave.

we can only control so much of who we are and who we let in. do not give power to the ones who want to change you. when you are ready, do it for yourself. once you do, no one will be able to stop it from happening. we are our own best chance of living a fulfilled life. one where the only promise broken, is that of a wish we made long ago about living for someone else before ourselves.

every day we have a choice to make.
i hope one of these days you choose
the love you need. i hope one of these
days you finally see the beauty in a face
i am looking at now and will never be
able to forget. there is a great power in
who you are. i just hope you never run
out on yourself before you see it, too.

i looked at you and saw the only reason i needed to give my soul to the art bursting inside of you. i saw magic for the first time in my life. ever since i was a kid, my mother told me about creatures like you. the ones who see brokenness and love even harder. the ones who can hold your hand and be holding every piece of the earth together at once.

there's nothing easy about going after what you want. scars heal. bruises fade. the body recovers. the heart beats on and on and on. the next step could lead you to the greatest dance of your life. may you only feel lost when the music stops. even after it does, sing your fucking heart out for the next adventure.

you are the love cried out by wolves. you are the life screaming out of me. you are the body i wish to lay with forever until this world ends and we begin again. you are the direct reflection of all oceans swimming in me; realizing how dreams can swim and never be taken under by what they do not see.

the best part about life is being your
own kind of weird and loving every
second of it without apologizing for
who you are. the first time you do,
will be the last time you ever feel
the wind catch you by surprise
with a winter's journal full of a
summer's goodbye.

i'll always be someone who pulls off on the side of the road, awaiting the moment to bloom. i am patient when it comes to savoring beauty. i am steadfast when it comes to holding in a breath, anticipating a wildness to appear where death remains stubborn and love is its mistress.

when i was a young boy, i would
scream into my pillow before i
went to sleep. i didn't want my
dreams to have my pain. i thought
if i could get it out of me, it would
be gone by morning. most of the
time the pillow woke up in tears
and other times it was the safest
place for me. when you are a child
with feelings left directionless,
you can only hope they find where
they need to go before they stay with
you your entire life, hoping you find
the way first.

the hell i once found myself in, reminds me of how endless tragedy can be when you never let out what was never meant to stay. we are not capable of producing anything more than pain when that is everything our hearts have known. but every once in a while, someone brave enough comes along and teaches us how to forget what life thought it beat into us.

your life will never get better if you are not actively
searching for things you love. i cannot tell you
how much you are going to suffer if you do not
do this. to be standstill, stagnate, and blind to
your own needs and feelings is a death sentence.
one that feels like living to those who know nothing
about it except routines and excuses. may you never
fall victim to your own way of life.

my heart doesn't belong here in this peace and quiet. at times, it's hard for me to make sense and even harder for me to think. the noise keeps my soul under, unable to break the surface with its grip holding onto the sky and who i used to be. i can still smell the cigarettes i put out on my arms back when pain was a game i always won. there is nothing left of the kid i was except for anger and regret for not being able to help the ones i loved the most. all the toys have been sold and laid down to rest in a room flooded by tears that got swallowed by the agony of being too young to know how to help myself. my life is not what i imagined it being back when they used to ask me what i wanted to be. i wish people would ask me now that i know. i still look around for my mother at times when i am hurting, even though i never saw her come to help me that often when i was young. there is still hope resting under my head that maybe one day i can believe her when she said she was. this life is still new to me. at times, i feel like a flower underneath a waterfall; all too much at once, but a necessary struggle to survive.

when you look into my eyes,
please see past the universe
you think exists in me.
i need you to realize that
without you seeing a life
together, my sky would
fall and surround me with
darkness from the space
that resides in my soul.
without you, i am nothing
more than a single particle
of love, desperately searching
for a heart that needs a human
to understand it.

there she was, holding her head as high
as a human possibly could. she always
loved to smell the fresh bloom of an
early morning. it was as if she came
to earth in order to love and
appreciate a life so many take for
granted. somehow, i managed to fall
into her atmosphere just in time for
her to save mine. she was such an
infectious spirit, and to know that
i was the one chosen to be there
when she woke up, made me believe
that heaven was always a dream she
brought to reality. a dream where her
blue eyes were the sky i had wished upon
to fall all over me, time and time again.

she gathered up all of her tears
and closed her hand around
them, making a fist of faith;
creating diamonds.

you should see the way she shines now.

i am deeply connected to everything, and with that, failure and heartache reach my bones as much as love and victory. i am still learning which one means more to me. i am still accepting not everyone will want what i offer. but to the one who truly does, i hope they understand what a bad day for me really is. i hope they understand my issues go well beyond the surface. well beyond a stone skipping over water you lose track of.

when i am done with my life, take me to the mountains and spread what's left of me amongst the giants. for they know who i am better than anyone else. they know the origin of where it all started long before my reason became apparent as to why my soul chose this body to use as a tool to carve out my spot in this cycle of repetitive breathing.

this version of me was built over the course of the hardest year of my life. it needed to be chaotic. i needed to know i could love myself through it. i needed to know i could survive and be a better human because of it. chaos knows me well, but i know it better. this next part of my life will challenge me unlike any previous one. struggling is what i am good at. i've done it my entire life, but through my struggle, i have found another chance to right my wrongs and take care of myself and those in my circle. i came back home to do just that. my life can wait.

being with you, it feels as though i am speaking to a mirror of my own soul. i have never met anyone else who could understand that reflection before. i have never met someone who could see themselves when looking back at me. someone who might be just as lost, just as broken, just as crazy to believe they can find love again.

i am going to write about you until words become stars and all of them are yours. i am going to be here until the last one falls for you and tells you how beautiful it was to be something more in your eyes. there are those we meet, lessons in the flesh, love in humanly bloom, that give our own life meaning. that give to us something no other ever could find in a million sunsets touching an ocean's love. we are destined for meetings. for encounters. for the unknown walks that lead us into some cafe or bookstore, and we find them. we find an honest answer as to why in the hell we have been hurting for so long when it seemed like no one cared to ask why. we blink and there they are one day. eyes that have seen nothing but ash and ruins, now see a human standing in it with them. they never ask what happened. all they do is help. they secure your beliefs in cosmic things. in the appearance of angels, sirens, and mermaids all gathered to help you from the place you were at. you may have never taken a breath and meant it until then. you may have written about a muse you only knew through your soul's truth. i'm going to make sure you never go a single day without knowing how fucking important you are not only to me, but to the existence we are living in. the world around me will know who you are and why i write the way i do. there is this magical thing about you i will keep to myself, but i will tell the world about you.

i am getting too old for the games these childish
humans play. jump ropes are only meant to hang
someone these days. no one ever sincerely says
how they feel, and if they do, no one gives a
shit, because they don't feel the same way
unless you have been sent to hell to reclaim
your soul. it isn't the human quality you look
for in someone else when lonely has been the
only thing you have known. it is the love you
once felt before them. the one that swore to
love you until it was all over. the one you still
hate yourself for loving today. all of it becomes
pointless if that love, that connection, that spark
isn't there.

i wonder often about our maybe. i wonder if you
were sent here to save me or kill me gently through
words backed up without actions. i wonder if you
ever see us during a sunset or sunrise, even though
i know your eyes love to stay in until the afternoon
is near. i wonder about the woman you want to be.
if this is the version of yourself you love the most,
or if there is still more of you left to explore.
i wonder if i will always give you goosebumps as
you do with me. it doesn't take much. just a gentle
nudge or slight touch can raise the dead buried
underneath my flesh. i wonder about you often.
it always leads me to the most beautiful and sincere
writing i can come up with. i hope it is enough when
that is all i have to give you.

we cry.
sometimes for pain and loss.
other times for joy and happiness.

we cry.
to cleanse the soul and years that had
once been who we were. to wash away
the old so that a future can rise again.

we cry.
for those who left and for those still
with us. life presents itself in all forms,
and i believe tears create stars.

we cry. we love. we live. we laugh. all for that
moment of reason. we do this because it is
needed. we do this because we were created
to form friendships and a lifetime worthy of
being complete.

we cry. but we are still young and alive. so shed
them and know you are not alone. we all feel.
some just chose to let others see it.

vulnerability is a superpower not everyone
is equipped with. be kind nonetheless
to those who do not carry its powers.

our life together is made up of honesty and always being ourselves with each other. when you have those two things, even the universe stops and stares with understanding that at times even humans can be more than just flesh and bones. they can be love. they can be alive amongst a field of dying flowers and still be a light to revive and save a tragedy from being permanent.

i've never witnessed the sky without the moon,
but lying here now, all of the stars are lonely
when you are not next to me. all i hear is
their cry when you are gone. sad eyes become
even heavier once you understand the ache
that is pulling them down.

i have been thinking a lot about how people meet and how connected we all are to the universe. some more than others obviously, but i know for certainty you and i are. i am not sure if it is about deserving each other or if it simply didn't know what to do with two souls who were created with so much fire and water. it's the way we met and how we are still here together that will always leave the lights on in the sky for those too blind to see how love has no plan. it only knows how to die and be reborn again under the same skin of earth we find ourselves standing on today. a piece which will always be closer to the heart of a star.

she never walked a mile in someone else's shoes.
she never had to. she wore heels. she is her very
own mile of madness. a walk nobody else has
taken. she likes it that way. she knows what it
takes to make magic, and therefore she is an
artist of life and chaos. coloring in the sun
where it is needed and using the watercolors
in her soul to make the rain fall when she
needs to dance. she is slowly moving,
but not all dreams dream the same.
not all humans need to rush through
what others will never experience.

the universe often at times is just a small world of

relative thoughts and unspoken words. sometimes

you get lucky and stumble upon someone who gets

your humor and adores you because you talk about

the stars as if wishes in fact live within them.

we closed our eyes and opened our hearts. it was a night where the insecurities of our souls died. in that moment, we became the bright light reflecting off of our skin. we were human, and that is the most beautiful conversation between two people who are getting to know what love feels like and forgetting what love once was.

the unknown is terrifying and completely paralyzing at times, but it's the one thing that keeps me fighting to be with you. i find peace and strength in things that frighten others. i find more life in things that are dead than those who say differently. not everyone knows what to look for when nothing was once all you had to live with and survive on.

she took a breath. not her first or last one, but one that ignited her most sought-after dreams. a breath made from hope, pain, love, and trust. it was hers and nobody would ever be able to take it away again. she was done settling for others. now, it is her adventure and we are merely stars caught in a web spun by a wanderlust lost to the wild.

maybe she wasn't the angel they all said she was. it didn't bother me, because i wasn't the devil most spoke of either. who we really are only matters to those who are willing to defy the push and pull of gravity surrounding our hearts.

when my hands find yours after a long and stressful day, only then do i feel as if i have accomplished something. between the hours of waking and lying down to rest, my arms are in dire search of you. when you go half the day without the one you love, you realize while holding them, just how easy it is to hold a world while forgetting about the one others are living in.

she knew it was important to be herself,

but that didn't mean she was filtered.

you cannot tame those who do not

value secondhand opinions and live

with an unquenchable thirst for

nothing less than wild.

with a smile that wrapped me up, she told me,
"thank you for riding the waves with me."

taking her hands, i squeezed them ever so
softly and pulled her closer to me, and said,

"the storms are worth it if you want the
rainbow. the sun always shines soon
after, sweetheart."

live life from the inside out with so much grit and persistence that even if it doesn't accept your terms, the end result will be the way you would want to be remembered.

she burns for a lot of things in life, but most importantly, she knows when to hold back the flames. there will be times when giving just enough, is actually too much. always respect yourself enough to know the difference.

the teacher asked, "what do you want to be when you grow up?" a simple question for some it may seem, though the little girl's answer made her classmates take notice and raise their hands as well.

"i want to be loved."

the life we try to find is sometimes the one we leave behind. but in order to live the seconds we are given, we must walk beyond the forest of the broken and continue smiling at the sun and dancing with the trees that are still standing.

i wish nothing else than for love
to find you. and when it does,
i hope it holds you and protects
you, releasing all the fear and
pain you have ever had to
endure. a moment of love
is a lifetime of freedom.

i cannot tell you what to do. i cannot tell you where to go. i will not tell you who to love. i will not tell you when to leave. but i will tell you the best way to swim is jumping into the water and submersing your fucking skull. using your arms and legs to travel the open sea in front of you, just got for it. take your breaths. take your time.

-do not rush magic. swim in its peace-

if you're going to break me, fucking break
me already. i am tired of walking on stars
for you when you won't even dance under
the moon for me. but here i stand with
both arms around my body, holding the
fragile pieces together patiently waiting
for you to leave. just know that when
you go, i will find the one who will
finally look at me as if i am not the
only one who is broken.

we talk to each other as much as life allows time
to stand still. it was in that moment i told her,

"even when we are not touching, we will always
be together."

that's what lovers do. they continually hold onto
the heart, while the rest of the world searches
for their own.

oftentimes we mistake our happiness with what makes up our life and we tear it all down because we feel like we don't deserve it. never mistake what's in your heart for who who is holding your hand.

we are all strange and mad. some of us though never have to wear masks to prove it. we walk around with our faces covered in it, unafraid of being seen out in public for the crazy ones we are. i will never tell my wolves to go and hide so your sheep can run free. i am already that way, and i will not change my appearance to make you feel better about yourself. i am done killing myself for others.

<u>be you.</u>

for there is no one else capable

of presenting the stars in such

an unexplainable way. for there

is no one else who the stars know

better. they have always been on

your side and in your eyes.

a shine like yours, that's all i

ever want to fucking know.

live your life for all the times you were told not to. we are not given many chances to try it for a second time. i have been in and out of my graves a few times, but not everyone gets to crawl back alive. please, live your fucking life and never hold back who and what you are. we live in a world that loves to cage and pen in wild creatures they don't understand. just as our hearts must be let out, too, and freed from dirty hands and souls who once thought they could hold something else that was not of their own.

there's a powerful beauty in the fire only those who have walked it can feel. there is nothing left for humans to consume once you have tasted its flames. you can always tell the ones who have. their eyes are full of unearthly things and get lost looking at a sunset which captures who they are and what they feel.

may the flowers bloom wherever your feet go
and wander. may they speak loving things to
you and be present in your time of need.
we are nothing more than everything that
has happened to us. allow their love to
guide the light you are desperately looking
for. their patience is a testament to who they
are. it is what makes them different from all
other living creatures.

chaos lives inside of me
and i am beginning to
embrace the chance for
something unexpected.

something entirely new to
touch me and allow me
to rest my hands when
all i had been waiting
for was the next fight.

breathe in the ocean. become the waves; always forward and with purpose. we are children of the moon and sun. wherever they go, you will find me with a beautiful truth about love and where it came from. you will find me burning stars to catch ambers from a song you once sung that they held inside of themselves. i am enthralled by your beauty. i know once your hand goes into mine and we are connected, nothing about this world will ever be the same for me. i cannot tell you how much i am looking forward to living and being around you first hand, first glimpse, first shade of red and orange we gather.

run with the lions and go as far as the mountains.
when you get there, tell the wild who you are.
tell everyone your story. do not hide behind your
tales of adventure. it gives us all hope that maybe
one day we can make our own footprints on the
moon or in the sand of some beach we have yet
to run on.

i'm finding it easier to breathe now that
i'm not breathing for you. now that
you no longer have a place in my life,
i can finally find a place to rest when
for too long i had been your leaning
post. now my back has a curve i am
trying to straighten out to make myself
more presentable in this humanly form
until i am walking with my truth to where
it belongs.

never apologize for being something other than human. not everyone knows the other side of life, but you do. you will always know where the moon runs to and why the sun screams out in his sleep. you are not made like the rest of us. you are not made from the same things that we are. i knew it the first time you told me your infatuation with moonish things.

hands bring the soul back to
life. a simple touch can change
someone's entire perception
of love. it has the power to
change an idea into a reality.
it has the power to transform
a dream into two eyes and
a heartbeat.

love is in the moments no one else sees but the soul. it is only present when you let go of the flesh and learn to appreciate the decorations inside of a human. however ruined one may be, it is what makes them who they are. even if you see christmas lights in May, there is still reason for celebration.

stay with me when the sun comes up. i am in need of another morning with you next to me. i am in need of an explanation as to how quickly day turns to night when you are the only living thing next to me. i am in need of your limbs to intertwine with mine until our branches reach the moon and tell her about the love we have learned from her and her lover.

i now know how the wolf feels.
i now know how a feeling can
unleash the deepest parts of
a soul and awake the bottomless
pits full of light and love, to bring
it up into the moonless nights.

<u>my moon</u>

you make me see things where
they should be. even when your
nakedness dances across a blue sky,
you were made to be seen holding
up all things that had once been
broken by fate's own hands.

there are versions of ourselves we have

yet to meet, and to me, that is the most

exciting part of life. the moment you

meet your best-self, your truest form

of soul, that is when you start believing

in the magic only a few will ever know

on an spiritual level.

i know i could do "this" by
myself, and when i say "this,"
i mean live, breathe, dream,
and wander.

but i am going to need you,
darling, in order to feverishly
love all of the things i just
listed above.

i still talk to you every night regardless of your distance from me. i know you hear me. i see it in your light. my curse is that i am lost to a feeling i may never get back again. it is what keeps me up with you. it is what keeps my eyes in my skull and my heart out of its cage.

when life gives you a moment, love it,
learn it, capture it. we go in search of
a million different things these days.
we all look for the next high, the next
bridge to burn, the next feeling to jump
from. but if we take our time with each
and every one of them, we will understand
more that if we wish for too long, everyone
we love will be gone. everything will be
buried next to those who we told it will
all be okay in time.

it is now, in this breath, in this deepest part of my lungs, i know who i am. there is no coward turning off the lights. there is no sheep to be seen running through these lands i tend to keep. there are only wild fucking beasts readying themselves for the next journey. for the next, i do, i vow to myself to keep. i cannot continue to runaway each time i feel the heaviness sit on my chest, waiting on me to say mercy. we come from the stars and i don't intend on letting them down anytime soon.

bright lights hit my face and sad sighs
take a place amongst kings and queens
rolling over graves with empty pockets;
nothing saved.

    save face my boy.

    save face, my girl.

    life is not a race to the end.

    it is a race to outlast it.

love isn't enough when the other human
you say it to, can only look away with
tears in their eyes, because they know if
they say it, they won't mean it. when it
happens, and it will, you must continue
on and force the next step in your journey.
life doesn't end with heartache. it only ends
with whatever we choose to carry along with
us. we were the pallbearers for our souls long
before being asked to be alive.

i wonder how the moon looks on you tonight.

i wonder if it gives you enough bravery to make

it through this fight. i wonder if lonely is lovely

or if it's only there for your light.

<u>adventure often and with intent.</u>

anything less than that and you are wasting your life. and to me, life is too fucking precious and short not to go out of your skin to chase down the wild you are in need of. for the remarkable moments that have yet to take place, make them something more to you and show up for yourself when it counts.

the night will always be where my
secrets make love to any truth they
can find. with any light they can feel.
with any resemblance of balance they
can sustain after gravity fights them
to maintain its hold on us all.

words never sleep alongside me. they will
be dead by morning then come back to
life once they hit paper. they are sleeping.
they are alive. they are human emotions
without a secret to keep or hold once
they become who you want them to be.

we have to learn which waves to surf and which ones
to ride out. only then can we understand the wave.
only then will we be able to speak the language
of her love and devotion to trek through the chaos
and meet us with calm. her gentleness reminds me
there are still things in me that need a name.

if i could tell you anything. if i could be honest for the rest of my life with you, you will need to know this about who i am and what i am wanting to give to you. you are the breath before life. you are the moment right before a sun is born again to love the moon in her space. this is what i offer for you. this is what and who you are to me. this love, this ever so fucking precious love i have for you, will never be wasted or misplaced.

life is about loving yourself during a time when no one else can. it is during that moment you will find if you have room to love anybody else. you will come to discover that solitude is a friend many never seek out, because being alone scares anyone not crazy enough to watch their demons sleep.

teach me about the things others have never wanted to learn about you. i am nothing more than a student of your soul. i have nothing but time and love to give. i am not here for theatrics or because someone told me something about you that made me feel differently. i am here because i want love to be wherever you are.

you have to keep going. you have to keep living each breath. it is our purpose in life to exhaust every particle that makes us who we are. some of us have faces that will never know themselves. i think that is the greatest tragedy in life; not seeing who you are until six feet is to high to climb.

we have yet to meet, and i am afraid "one day" will never make it to us. i am afraid of the smallest of fears living within this world. i am aware of whatever is meant to be, will be. we are different devils and angels than those before us. we are raging fires and rapids, all consumed in living a meaningful life. you are the only woman i have ever imagined running away with and adventuring until our bones grew tired from the flesh it kept alive for all those years we stayed out too late; weathering along with the cosmos and giving light back to the night.

we are all deserving of what makes us better humans. we are all deserving of someone who stays not because they have to and not because we ask them, but because they choose a life with us. because they see life together means being able to have their best days ahead of them with you there to make each one mean something more than before. may what you seek out be prepared to take on what is inside of you. the ones who find you, will be with you long after your light dies out and becomes another guiding force to use on the other side.

i don't know who you are yet, but i am looking forward to the chance of one day sitting down with you and telling you how far i have traveled just to hear your questions about life and love. to see the struggles you wear so i can help ease them off of you. to let you know i have seen a million different kinds of light, but none of them looked like you. none of them penetrated my soul quite like the night we stood under the same moon, in different states, and told each other every truth we had disguised as lies to keep the other safe. i don't know who you are yet, but this new moon is showing me how beauty is best seen when it shines on you.

my loneliness isn't a reflection of my needs. it's just what i am comfortable with. i am still unfamiliar with company, with humans staying too long. with thoughts coming over without revealing what they want. with dreams too real for my soul to feel. with nightmares caught in my bones and separating heart from home. i am in need of nothing, though your everything could change my entire perception of what it is to be in love. of what it is to have someone replace your comfort and make it even more unbearable to be without someone you love.

i didn't look for you to save me. i just
wanted to know if you would leave or
stay. hesitation only makes things easier,
and when you paused for me, it was all i
needed to know you would be the next
stranger i would have to say goodbye to
and never cross paths again. life is funny
thing. we meet thousands of humans every
day, whether we realize it or not. each one
with a story like yours. each one looking
for some type of connection so they know
how it feels to be heard. being in love is
a strange fucking thing, but one i hate
when the one you are with becomes
one of those you have to keep passing
along your way to a new life.

humans stay longer in our hearts than in our lives,
because sometimes, it's the only way to remember
them while they are here. not every visit is meant
to be forever, but there is nothing in this universe
with a better memory than a heart. which is why
i can still feel you in my shallow breaths or when
the moon looks at me in a way that can leave me
feeling wholesome. energy remains residual
long after the initial encounter. my entire life
is made up of brokenness disguised as something
i carry around to shield me from others. but it
is only thing i have that hasn't left me for
something it felt to be better than who i am.

you are only replaceable to those who cannot find themselves. it is not your job or duty to become someone they need in order to be a better version of who they are. we cannot be caregivers to the able and living. it only takes us away from our purpose.

you read of a universe that is prospering. one made from
seagoing life and hunters on the prowl. you smell of newly
opened books and freshly picked moon light. you feel as
soft as a thought being born that doesn't know how cruel
the world can be, but still full of common sense knowing
the world will never change, regardless of what you believe.
you are the imagination of every living thing underneath
the earth's roof. your power is infinite and has been
sculpted by knowledge found where many never have
time to stay for long or choose to remain. but you, you
are undoubtedly the single most thought about human
i will ever wish to or hope to think about. you make me
brave enough to be myself.

the earth will never be able to mirror the true beauty inside of you. it is only fair that you look and stay looking at the moon. not for comparison, but a true reflection of self and soul. she is your mother and you are her daughter of shine and glimmer.

i make room for who you are as a woman and soul. your entirety has always been welcomed in my life. it will continue to serve me as inspiration as to where life began and where love was ultimately discovered. i have always needed you to be the words i never had the courage to type until now. your resiliency built this structural image i will continue to add to.

it is all about the smell of a new month and new moon, and i am opening myself up to all of it. i am tired of being shelved and saved for later. i am exhausted of being returned for something more than what i offer. i am worn out, not by love, but by what others see love to be.

be sure to live with laughter.
it has been known to cure
any ache you have.
even if it is the furthest
thing from a real one,
practicing anything enough
makes you believe you can.

i'm trying to remove my feelings so i can understand yours. adding anything else to an already discarded pile is pointless if what you are getting rid of is the same color, feeling, emotion, action. i remove all of who i am in order to understand the parts of you no one else ever could or did.

baby steps eventually turn into wings. the further we go in life, the more hurt we may feel. the more love we may give. the more hope we may uncover underneath whatever it is we believe in. i need you to know being brave has nothing to do with what you are capable of. it is going forward in this journey, accepting yourself for all faults, all insecurities, all of what others never could tell you was there, but you never quit on telling yourself once you arrived and saw it.

i'll stand in the middle of the street if
it means getting one picture out of a
hundred just right. i will do the same
with you. day or night, i will make damn
sure you are okay with whatever it is you
are feeling. being here with you means
more than experiencing the good with
you. it is taking in all the bad and turning
it into a beautiful moment, because you
have gone too long not knowing what the
moon looks like at night when you have
had to hide your face in order to escape
the pain of not feeling like you are enough.
when we both know how many lies it takes
before a single truth is told.

wherever the journey takes you, be
there entirely. we as humans get
too much in a hurry these days.
we always want the next best thing.
the next piece of new technology.
the only upgrade needed is the one
that makes you stop for a second,
collect your breath, and see how
goddamn magical it is being alive
and present in your own life. we are
the next best thing for someone who
has been without everything.

amongst the city lights, i still see you.
the flicker you see is that of a soul
who is lost, but can still bend around
the universe and take on the moon's
grace and vulnerability; she is all magic.
even if you can't see it, you will start
believing in its feeling again.

maybe one day i will find whatever it is i am after. maybe one day it will be somewhere with you. maybe one day it will be a life i once thought i didn't deserve until you told me and showed me just how romance can be nothing more than a closeness when the lights go out.

sometimes i forget all of the pain,

then beauty sneaks into tell me

there is more to life than feeling

everything i do and everything

others never can.

we will have our day. a day that will know all about our love. a day that will serve us long after these bodies grow tired of keeping in our souls and give them infinite wander to call a home.

when someone asks who i am,

i tell them to look up to the

moon. she will always have

the best parts of me.

one day at a time. tomorrow will be better, because today showed me proof. today gave me you and left sorrow out in a field to die alone. it was a place i had been before. alone and on my own with nothing more than hatred and anger to keep me warm and leaving me feeling ashamed. but not today. not with this new emotional color i have in my heart and eyes for you. there is a new me, where death no longer asks me when. it simply leaves me alone to live and breathe with you.

there you are. still giving me life during the day.
still giving me a breath to take when my lungs
have only known of loss. when they have been
holding in and holding onto someone who said
they would be there and would be right back once
they found what they were looking for. it is safe to
say that to save my own fate, she left me for good,
and i am now in the company of someone who
loves me because staying means more to us both
than searching out reasons to leave.

every last drop of light, i will find.
unlike the ones before us, we know
the night doesn't always win. there is
sweet victory in the eyes of those who
have seen defeat and know what it is
like to be left broken and shattered by
those no better than who we needed
them to be at the time of our inability
to decide on our own that we were
fucking enough, even if our bones
broke from being made of stone.

holy fires and sacred truths come out of you.
i have been around thousands of humans
that were nothing more than their own
shadows. i am too old for anymore games
or light-tricks. i am too old for meaningless
conversations and hollowed out feelings.
it won't be long until i am home and you
become a holy ground i walk above to never
mistreat you or misstep onto an emotion to
cause you pain or make you retreat back into
the walls we had once conquered together.

i believe in seeing things others never pay
attention to. everyday, my eyes are grateful.
everyday, i am finding more things i never
knew i could love and learn to appreciate.
i haven't always treated myself kind in my
own eyes, but you are showing me a
different side of who i am. you are making
me look behind them where my darkness
is and confronting it all. not once have you
forced me to open them when i wasn't ready.
and to me, that is the singular thing i love
most about you.

wherever you are, i hope it is a place that assists your growth and never impedes your dreams. we are all looking for some type of shelter. be it in another human, a field of the wildest wild flowers, or in some abandoned cave we can make our own and paint all of the walls whichever color we want. there is safety in loss that we don't understand until we try and add to it. there is something magical about a human who is pure vulnerability stripped to its core, asking for something more than the occasional safety net to catch them. i am all hands, arms, legs and feet, stumbling around as if i know what it all means. the funny thing is, i am not seeking definition.
i am after something that can remain undefined, but still count as something to remember.

you are beginning to change me and how i see love. my hands are restless, just as my soul; always moving with an intent to end up within yours. deep breaths keep my body inflated, as the world around me rotates a little more to see you differently. i am not sure what i am after anymore, but i am yours when you are ready. i'll be yours, infinitely.

i miss you. it's weird, because i have never met you, but in another world, another life, our souls exchanged stars. i'm unsure of when or if i will ever see you and hold you, but just know i walk this path in hopes of running into you when we both least expect it. moments like that make us love with a purpose greater than the ones we all think we have already.

there are so many things i would love to tell you and show you. they are never shared because i have been too afraid of what is living behind my walls. it has been so long since i have stepped foot outside the safety of hope, but i am going to break through to the other side for you. i now know i will never be able to stay away from you once there is nothing but light to love you in.

i have traveled across distant skies and over the hearts of many, because contact with certain people make me anxious and i do not know whether i should bleed myself of sin or welcome them in. i am off the drink and feeling alive for the first time since my little heart was a baby. a heart conceived by fate combined with our encounter long ago before flesh ever knew bone. it is how homes are made.

where we go from here is between us and the courage embedded in our bones. and if we must carry it a bit further to reach who we need to be, i shall break every part of my structure until love finally stands again.

if there ever comes a time when you cannot taste my soul or remember how my eyes held you, please, my love, come back to me and i will show you again. if you are unable to find me, take time with yourself until you are able to see who it is you want to become. i would wait a thousand moons to see the singular one i cannot live without.

i'm tripping over stars again, hopelessly wandering out of my comfort zone to see how far away time for us actually is. hoping there is no such thing as maybe or a pause. hoping wherever it is, our hands learn how to fit into spaces only we can connect.

it's okay if you feel lost and out of place. i have always told you that you are special and unique, just as the moon is when you can see her during the day. own it, sweetheart. you are the magic around each and every one of us.

i hope you find someone who only wants the best for you. who checks on you not for any reason particular, but just wanting to make sure you are okay so they can be. someone who loves the stories you tell about your past and doesn't judge based on their outcomes. someone who wakes up before you while you sleep next to them. never touching, but merely being there gives them strength to keep going. they never want to wake you, unless it is because of a nightmare they had and need reassurance it wasn't real. to make sure they didn't lose you in-between dreams. someone who wants nothing more than to make a single promise of loving you you until all that is left to love is your soul. someone who wants you and notices you and the small changes you make in your appearance to see if they are paying attention. all of this i hope for you, i wish for you. because in the end, it is about who loves being with you through all the bullshit and makes sure you are okay not just some of the time, but all of the time. it is a series of questions where you hope there is no hesitation between answers.

some things are just better lived for a short while. anything longer can ruin the magic of a moment. anything longer can completely remake the structure of who we are, and i am not brave enough to walk around in circles looking for my heart again. i am not brave enough to reach out for reds and   and pinks, only to grab onto someone who doesn't believe in the colors we call love. only to grab onto the one who doesn't bleed the same way i do.

i'm not yours, and it still hurts to feel it. it still hurts to say it. it still hurts to know it. it still hurts being me without you. but each day i am learning a new piece of who i am. i am learning why you needed to go and leave me where you left me. i know it wasn't out of spite or careless behavior. you just had a plan before you told me about it. and that's okay. i am learning now that i am better without you. i am learning what love can be when two humans actually fucking care about what happens at the ending.

she asked me, "how does a soul die?"

i thought about it for a few minutes, because i knew it was an honest question, and with honest questions, you need a proper and meaningful reply.

"by holding back what it feels. by loving what doesn't love it back. by pretending to be present, all the while living a totally and completely different life."

she smiled, and said, "thank you." i kissed her forehead and told her, "now you know how to kill me if you ever need to."

we both laughed and went on about our day with more conversations that attracted me to her in the first place. her mind is still my favorite part about her. her wit and endearing approach to life is the sexiest thing my soul has ever felt.

i believe we all have our own personal dance with
darkness. those willing to fight and make it out,
do their best to light whatever way they can for
those who need it. and to the ones who never
make it out, still become a light in a sky for us
who need a reminder why we keep fighting
and why the battle never fucking ends. be light
or become a shelter for it. we all need both when
it is all said and done.

the miles that separate us only tell us how far we need to go to meet them there. they should never be a reason why it doesn't work. just ask the sun and moon. pay attention to what fucking matters in this world and you will never be in the wrong for going the extra mile for someone who would never think anyone ever could based on the actions of those before you. we all deserve someone who wants us to be happy. we all deserve someone who wants to give their best effort at doing such a thing.

love is knowing you will be there in the morning before the sun touches our windows. love is knowing how long you have waited to be the reason someone smiles after the day tried to steal away their shine. love is the truth behind the night. love remains until bones become dust and drifts away into the cosmos to be found again by someone seeking affirmation of its existence.

i always adored her for the way she showed up each day not always feeling her best, but choosing to be herself regardless of feeling or emotion. to be comfortable in your own skin is not an art. it is a promise to keep.

you were my forever muse. i once thought i could never write about anything but you. i showed you my writings first before anyone else because your opinion and suggestions were my favorite part of my day. it was the greatest joy and heartbreak of once was something i looked forward to every day. my white whale. my moon. my nothing but a memory. you were once so many things, but now all you are is a life i am forgetting. i write this knowing you are gone and have been gone for years now. it is time i follow suit. strangers are nothing more than humans who lost each other along the way. all the broken in this world feel the same. we who know heartache, know beauty to be a sad face that once carried your smile.

i have never had a memory hold me as close as the one i have of you. it is the flower that will never die. but time does us no favors holding onto things meant for something else. i can only hope this keeps the moon above me before it, too, falls below my chest.

i hope you find someone who brings out the best in you without taking away from the human you are. someone who loves each and every flaw you speak of, but still finds beauty in it all. someone who loves you on your worst days and keeps you balanced on your good days. i hope you find them without expectations, without something to prove to someone else who said you never could. i hope they give you peace when the noise overtakes your joy, your smile, and a heart that doesn't always know what it wants.

i have learned a million different things throughout my life and have forgotten just as many. but i will never forget when time taught me that pain is what we make it. that pain can be beautiful, too, if given a chance to prove it is worth feeling.

not all promises are made to be kept. some last just long enough for you to know it was meant to happen and you are a better human because of it. there are no such things as happy endings. there is only what we make of our life and love after we close the book.

i have been taught love by everyone i have
met, whether in passing or commitment.
i can only hope its teachings continue to
inspire my heart in ways i will one day
fully grasp.

at the end of my life, even if i have

no one there with me to share it,

i will always have the comfort and

light of the moon.

i'm tired most days, but not exhausted. i am in love some days, but not every second. my life is and has been a series of mistakes and myself forgiving others for half of my life. i never really tell others how they make me feel when they hurt me or leave me or never call. i honestly don't see the point of it.
i never want someone else to have that power over me, that distinct control over my emotions. i have never been good at staying in one place for that long. i never want to be comfortable unless it is my time to welcome it into my life. i haven't arrived there yet. i am still a creep lurking in my own life. i am still a loser who hasn't got anything right except sitting at my desk and typing. i feel safe here. i feel at home here. i feel like i finally take on my name and take off all emotions and i am happy. my worst is worse than yours. my insane will never be kissed by any right minded woman. i am okay with it all because i know who i am. but that doesn't mean i have figured it out. my arms search for you. my eyes search for light. my mind searches for chaos. my soul searches for anything regarding a guarding of gardens and restoring anything that is broken. it is why i spend so much of my time in solitude. it is the only place i know of that can handle who i am.

my whole life i have been waiting for someone like you. if waiting has taught me anything, it is that no matter how long you do it, nothing is wasted if you gave your best when you had nothing else to give.

i am as lonely as the birds that never rise. my attempt to love is that of a summer's serenade. it only lasts for as long as you can bare your soul until a change takes you away in hopes of returning with something different to offer.

as much as it hurts, i know you will find someone who isn't me and i will smile when you do if you haven't already and know how happy you are. someone who will be able to give you more than i ever could. you gave me the best years of my life thus far and it has been more than anyone else ever has given back to me. when someone asks me,

"what happened to you?
you look so different."

i will look for you and tell them, "she did."

love will be everything that reminds

me of you. i will never be without

its moments. i will never run out

on you. i will never run out of you.

a heart breaks differently when there is no one
else around to hear it. you can hear the screams
and cries from all of your emotions. the ones
you kept inside before showing your smile.
the ones you showed before you were ready
to undress your fears to someone who was
still fully clothed in theirs. a heart never fully
repairs itself unfortunately. we all have that
one crack, that one split, that one arrow that
leaves its mark which will never hold love again.

you have lost me completely. if i do not let go of the

slack i have given you, it will hang me, and i am not

ready to die just yet for someone who doesn't love

me like i loved you. who doesn't feel the same way

as i do when the moon is above us.

it was my fault. i was already on one knee before i met you. i fall in love before it knows me. i am too much soul for common earth life. i am too lost to be found. i am too much chaos for the hurricane you believe yourself to be. i am too much for anything these days.

i am always wishing for a subtle nudge from all the uncertainty i feel at times. maybe then i could fall like an idiot onto my face for others to see how human i can be. other times i wish i could stumble into a lover and look at her and not feel as if i am not good enough to even be around someone as beautiful as the moon. my nerves are shot. my limbs hang below the surface, afraid to swing to another star. i am caught in midair. i am caught with words meant for her, but unable to speak. i wake up nervous and go to bed with trepidation i may never get another chance to tell her i am sorry for my way of saying hello.

you never enjoyed being told what to do.
your free spirit has made you into a dream
for some and a reality to those who you let
in. you have built yourself a beautiful life
and i hope the moon is always allowed in.
i hope she shines for you. i hope she tells
you how loved, rare, and special you are.
my eyes have seen broken, and even in
that state of being, you are still magic.
you are still whole enough to find
yourself again, sweet soul.

heartache made me who i am. if i know anything, there is still a love out there to be held close and told how precious it still is. there are those we hold onto, because a force beyond our control deems them to be someone to remain with us for the rest of our lives. take it as a sign, an unrequited attempt of surrender, as things continue to unfold for you in this life we all think gives us nothing in return. when it is untimely with its grace and forgiveness.

hello, june.

i am still here and that's a victory for me.
people will enter and exit your life with
or without reason. it isn't up to you to
figure out why. just accept what is and
what isn't. life is simple once you begin
to stop worrying about those who never
worry about you. move forward with
kindness in your heart for where you
are and who you are. i will be okay.
it has taken a lot of pain and
heartbreak to make me, me.

she asked me, "how do you know when fighting for what you want and fighting for love is over?"

it felt like i had deja vu. i had been asked this before by every woman i was once in love with. they all ended so i could only assume the same fate for us.

i stepped forward, grabbed her hands, and gently spoke what i have learned first hand.

"when you are the only one fighting for it all without the other ever lifting a hand. when they become motionless for emotions. when you find yourself more in love with the idea of them than who they are when they are with you."

we all have our reasons for leaving. we all fight demons not all can see. we all love in our own way. we are cursed with it all the day of our birth. our journey is to find love, make love, and be love. however it happens in whatever order, i know something like that exists even if it is never meant to stay in my heart longer than the doubt keeping it warm.

i once thought you were sent to save me.
now i know you were just another demon
i needed to face. victory looks different for
everyone. a few times in life, you can simply
walk away and that be the biggest battle you
have ever won. i am proud i can say i did
that with you. i am proud i didn't leave my
body on the battlefield to die and rot like i
had before. you almost killed me, but i need
to die for someone better. not for someone
who just wanted me gone.

and if you never come back to me, as least i will know you made it home. wherever and whomever that is, i will know you are safe. that is and was my biggest concern. now i can make sure i do, too.

tipsy like a watered rose, she walks
with the stars and speaks of a time
before this. a time when humans
only needed a little extra love to
know it would be okay. a time
when you stayed, because love
never made you do anything
you didn't want to do.

everybody wants to fix your broken, until they, too, become what they tried to save. until they become too much of who you are and need someone else who is not you.

-repetition without change is also called death-

there's a place where angels hide and
demons die. where birds rise without
fear and strangers never are without
love. a place where blood covers
mountains and light penetrates
light. we must go. our feet, they run.
our arms, sturdy with fight. our fists,
bang like drums set upon the moon.
eyes never blink at a chance to seek
the riches we all hope to find.
we must go. it is all that's left now.

my soul knew it was you. all i had to do was to allow those feelings to exist within my body. within my humanly form. everything else i feel, is just a reciprocal emotion, being emoted by two lovers who waited out a world to be born to find each other again.

before the day can speak, i say your
name. not in prayer or remembrance,
but in a holy fucking love. you have
always been the devil's heartache.
you have always been the break in
my voice when pain tries to take
me away. you have always been
how i get back to myself.

there is still life to be lived. there is still love to be wished for. there is still a heart to be heard. there is still more to figure out and leave behind. my roots may never know how to take and release, but i am only destined for where i find myself between the death and growth of my needs. the time lapse between child of exile and human of his own home. a roof may never hold me more than a single year at a time, but as long as i am below this light, all things are cared for within. all things are where they should be, even with a heartless mind and hungering pains.

the best advice i can give you,
is to always trust your intuition.
it is how the soul speaks to all
of us. it is the carrier of all
things precious and vital which
keeps our eyes opened and our
hearts free. learn to appreciate
its teachings and you will be
safe from life's undoing.

days pass before me. breaths of those behind me. days last for a split second. months fade into the backseat. whispers of those around me catch me like mountains embracing a new day. years slip between my teeth. tears of those in front of me. decades lose sleep, and before you turn around, change is your new best friend.

we are destined for the stars if we believe in the magic residing within our dreams. it feels like i have been in a cosmic state since i was born. while others hang their heads, mine has been fixated on the mother above us, keeping more than just her light on. as long as i can see her, i know everything that is supposed to happen to me, will. trust is a bond between human and its soul. anything more than that, you are giving too much. if you are expecting more in return before you are honest with yourself, the universe in you will collapse.

the only choice we have is how much love
we give and how many times we are able
to accept it in return. we are made to
believe there is more to life than that.
but when it is all said and done,
it is the only fucking thing keeping
us from completely breaking apart.

maybe it was love. maybe it was loss, maybe it was me. maybe it was you. maybe it was the moon. maybe it was insanity. maybe it was hunger. maybe it was the color of your bones. maybe it was something more. maybe it will forever be a fleeting feeling we will never get again. maybe if we do, we can hold on a little longer next time.

some days i still retreat. not because of
what i cannot control, but because it is
who i am. i run off with myself to collect
my thoughts. it is nothing against those
in my life. i just need safety in numbers,
and that will always be one. my lessons
are only learned through pain.

and goddamn, have i been crying out for mercy.

i will always be searching for something, and that is the center of who i am. there are times i still have no clue as to what i am doing here, but if i take a moment and pause with the sun, i can see my shadow as a constant and still with me. only in loneliness, do we find true companionship.

i am more than wild. i am an untamed
star. i am a beast hiding behind this
planet. i am a creature made from
another time. as i sit here with feelings
in my hands that i cannot choke out,
i look up to see if she is there. to see if
she still sees me as i see her. the moon
remains full for me, because she still
loves me after everything i have done.
there is not another i will love as much.

i love you, but i haven't met you yet. i know once we meet, what i am feeling now will bring the moon back to me. i know my words will be full of love again. i know when we do see each other, our souls will look at us smiling, and tell us,

"we told you so."

i still get nervous around humans who have yet
to experience life. they talk without an ache in
their voice. they speak without hiding behind
words they don't believe in. they only step
outside when it suits them to. they have
never jumped out into an unknown feeling.
they simply discard anything that isn't to their
liking. they sit there with doors closed when
a beautiful moon is on display for them to
love. maybe they love differently. maybe they
were not made for change. they watch the
same flowers die each day, but are sure to
drink first when thirst overtakes their bodies.
we as humans have become numb to our
own reflexes and wonder why we only care
when things do not go as planned.

i am still learning how to love myself. i am still searching for adventures and words that are beyond my grasp. i am still settling into my bones and doing my best to make this place a home. i am a forever wanderer, with a heart that holds more love these days than the ache it once held. i am growing older, which is something i would never get the opportunity to do. i am still getting used to the face i see in the mirror, and i hope it continues to look back with gratitude and grace.

i lost it all, but i will be as wild as i can if it means having you next to me. there is only safety in the stars and moon, for you and i. there is nothing else in this world for me if strangers cannot make an attempt at learning each other again. there is not a soul in this world i haven't felt in some way. it is why my body shakes at the thought of any goodbye. it is why i cannot let go of the fight.

i would wait forever to spend just one night with you to know it was all worth it. to know you are there, enjoying the same intimacy we call love. to know you are there smiling back at me when we both catch ourselves laughing at our child-like minds during an "adult" conversation. what we have made ours, will never be someone else's. forgetting takes too much energy for me these days and that is the last thing i will use it on.

i hope you find someone who will be there at
3am when you feel your thoughts are making
it impossible to rest. i hope at 3pm the next
day, they are still trying to love you the same.
we deserve someone's best at all times,
though we should never have to ask for it.
the first time you do, will be the last time
you get a mutual response.

it takes more than light to know darkness.
it takes more of you to understand parts
of me. at times, i can be nothing more
than a shadow with bones, but you bring
out the human in me. you bring out the
words i have kept behind the moon so no
one would ever know where i found you.
i am not one to give away my secrets, but
you make it impossible not to want to give
you more of the things i have been saving,
hoping you would one day find them again.

some days, all i can do is look out at what's around me, and hope wherever you are, you see it with me, too. some days, i can speak for hours or be as silent as a night that forgot how to howl. it is all surreal to me when these fugitives disguised as my own feelings begin to find new space to wander. i am not too entirely sure as to how they get from one place to another going undetected, but i am thankful freedom welcomes them when their bodies become weary.

there is still magic to be made and dreams to chase. you are on your way to where the ocean drinks the stars and memories never grow old. you were made to be you. this is the moment you have waited for your entire life. please do not waste it on maybe. please do not waste it on an undeserved second chance that will break your fucking heart.

i am after something not found on this planet.
i am a visitor with wings, afraid of grounding
themselves for too long. i talk in stars and speak
a language forgotten by the humans who roam
these lands. maybe one day i will learn their ways.
but in all honesty, i hope i never do. i would much
rather keep my form than be turned into something
i am not. i enjoy watching others who are unsure of
what they see or know. the mystery makes the soul
rare, and rare i shall remain.

maybe love is nothing more than finding it
in someone who doesn't have the strength
to find it within themselves. we are made
to believe in something we have a difficult
time finding under our own bones. love is
easy, they say. love is poignant, they say.
love is the fiber of truth in a soul's breath,
i tell them. love is the devil's heart breaking,
knowing the flames don't scorch your truth.

take a few moments to roam with the
flowers and learn the language of their
softness. may they teach you how to
remain human, to remain still long
enough to appreciate the light where
it stands. may love always be the reason.
may it always be a gentle reminder placed
on lips, hands, and a forehead that adores
your effortless ways of making them feel
more than they ever have before.

creation is the key to all things living and dead. we are all but a centerpiece built from bone and rivers. we dance in melodies and speak an easy tune made from a mother's heart and a father's restored praise in his child. our energies are felt best through an open wound and nothing that makes sense will ever be found there. kiss me and hold me close. tell me everything is okay. tell me everything is good. i was raised by a liar and a cheat, so forgive me if the floor kisses my knees and presses against the lies i have stomached for too long, tap dancing to holy things. drinking and throwing back our holy water, we are not the crown of thorns, dear child. we are the rose.

bury me deep into the earth. water me with
light. may i grow to be everything you see.
may i live in the places your heart beats.
may i be so lucky as to be the first word
spoken by the sun that finds you after a
long day. may i be everything you need
when night approaches and you feel
an uneasy attempt of sleep on its way.

i will grow for you, if you will stay alive for me.

i'm still learning how to be human. how to be myself. how to love what i see. how to enjoy what i have made. how to enunciate my truth. how to allow others to help me. how to stay centered when my soul remains constantly in motion. it takes great patience to be me. and i am okay with that. life has taught me how to hold my breath, but still breathe in other ways.

you are energy. you are light. you are love in
every season. you are adventure. you are grace.
you are home to my boners. you are wild.
you are ambitious. you are all things precious.
you are galaxies. you are present. you are in love
with every minute. you are a gentle embrace of
chaos for those who have missed out on their
own. you are freedom. you are set free. you are
above all, everything to me. stay young in
everything you do and all the places you go.
a soul never forgets the moon, and she will
always remember the human who never gave
up on one of her own.

all of us are born with some type of ache. but not everyone

knows it to be love. we drink and smoke and laugh away

at any thought it could be anything more, because for some

of us, the fucking ache never dies. it stays long after we are

gone, in the lives we were too foolish and coward to live.

it stays in those we were too scared to love the right way.

love is everything. it is the beginning of
mindless madness. it is the tip of chaos.
it is on angel's wings set above a red
moon. we are all stories and colors
that make life believable. speak to
me in purples and greens. speak
to me in ocean's lyrics to the sea.
sing for me a song of peace.

                              sing for me, anything,

i have been pushed to my limits. though it didn't
completely break me, it cracked just enough who
i was for me to see where i need to strengthen
myself. only at our breaking points, do we
find how unbreakable the rest of our life is.

love me as i am. with broken faces building a smile over the course of a life that never seemed real to me before you. love me as i am. i am still learning how to say your name, but all i know about life is love. all i know about you, is that love knows me better because of who you are.

there is magic in the broken.
there is love in the hopeless.
there is beauty in the pieces.
there is a woman within
the warrior who sheds all
armor to feel human
once again.

find someone who loves you for all of your
mistakes. for all of your weirdness. for all of
the things that make you different. even love
itself is fucking crazy. we begin as strangers,
who by chance meet and go one these things
called dates to get to know one another.
and over time, those dates may or may not
accumulate into one specific date where our
families become one. love is a lot of things.
but most importantly, it is true, understanding,
and compassionate for all that comes with the
simplistic or chaotic tendencies around your
heart, mind, and soul. do not bow your head
in shame because of what has happened to you.
allow yourself to stand tall amongst the rest of
those who are either liars or scared to love the
broken. keep walking and you will come across
someone who will hold you the way you have
always needed to be held.

www.ingramcontent.com/pod-product-compliance
Lightning Source LLC
Chambersburg PA
CBHW021948290426
44108CB00012B/988